GARDEN GUIDES

SHRUBS & TREES

p^3

Garden Guides

Shrubs & Trees

Vroni Gordon

Illustrations by
Elaine Franks

This is a P³ book
This edition published in 2003

P³
Queen Street House
4 Queen Street
Bath BA1 1HE

Produced by
Robert Ditchfield Ltd

ISBN 1-40540-586-4

A copy of the British Library Cataloguing in Publication Data is avaliable from the Library.

Printed in Italy

Acknowledgements

The publishers would like to thank the many people and organizations who have allowed photographs to be taken for this book, including the following:

Bromesberrow Place; Burford House, Tenbury Wells; Lallie Cox, Woodpeckers, Marcliff, Bidford-on-Avon; Dinmore Manor; Richard Edwards, Well Cottage, Blakemere; Frampton Manor; Lance Hattatt, Arrow Cottage, Weobley; The Hop Pocket, Bishops Frome; Mr and Mrs R. Norman, Marley Bank, Whitbourne; The Picton Garden, Colwall; Powys Castle (National Trust); Mrs Clive Richards, Lower Hope, Ullingswick; Royal Botanic Gardens, Kew; RHS Garden, Wisley; Sissinghurst Castle (National Trust); Raymond Treasure, Stockton Bury Farm, Kimbolton; Wakehurst Place (National Trust); Wyevale Garden Centre, Hereford.

Contents

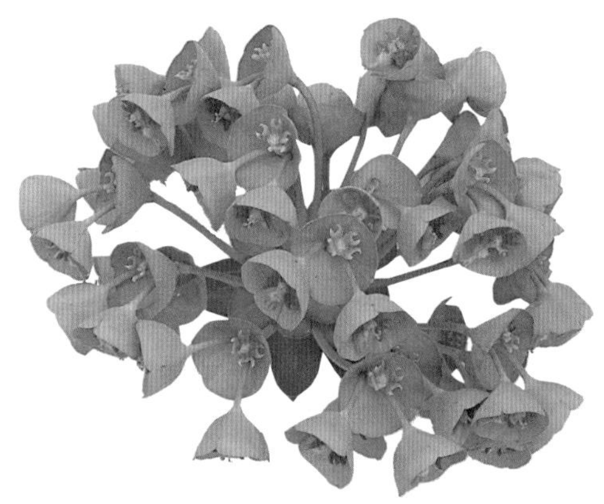

Poisonous Plants

In recent years, concern has been voiced about poisonous plants or plants which can cause allergic reactions if touched. The fact is that many plants are poisonous, some in a particular part, others in all their parts. For the sake of safety, it is always, without exception, essential to assume that no part of a plant should be eaten unless it is known, without any doubt whatsoever, that the plant or its part is edible and that it cannot provoke an allergic reaction in the individual person who samples it. It must also be remembered that some plants can cause severe dermatitis, blistering or an allergic reaction if touched, in some individuals and not in others. It is the responsibility of the individual to take all the above into account.

How to Use This Book

Where appropriate, approximate measurements of a plant's height have been given, and also the spread where this is significant, in both metric and imperial measures. The height is the first measurement, as for example 1.2m × 60cm/4 × 2ft. However, both height and spread vary so greatly from garden to garden since they depend on soil, climate and position, that these measurements are offered as guides only. This is especially true of trees and shrubs where ultimate growth can be unpredictable.

The following symbols are also used throughout the book:

- ❍ = thrives best or only in full sun
- ◐ = thrives best or only in part-shade
- ● = succeeds in full shade
- E = evergreen

Where no sun symbol and no reference to sun or shade is made in the text, it can be assumed that the plant tolerates sun or light shade.

Plant Names

For ease of reference this book gives the botanical name under which a plant is most widely listed for the gardener. These names are sometimes changed and in such cases the new name has been included. Common names are given wherever they are in frequent use.

Shrubs and Trees

There is little need to ask why trees and shrubs are so important in our landscape and in our gardens. Because of their woody trunks and stems the hardy ones survive winters and can go on growing year after year and so they are our most constant and faithful companions. Their framework – even if they have lost their leaves – is still visible in the winter when most of the perennials, the colourful annuals and the bulbs have died down or been dug up, when even the grass may have disappeared under a blanket of snow.

Because they stay with us not only throughout the year but over many years, some becoming the largest plants of all, it is to trees and shrubs we turn to provide the permanent shape of the garden – to form the living 'walls' and the most important 'furniture'. They can be used as a background, but they can also star in their own right, giving us pleasure with their leaves, flowers, berries, hips, bark and scent. Yet again, whenever there is a special need – something to grow in a difficult spot, for instance – we can be sure that a plant can be found to meet it.

A composition that exploits differences in colour and shape. On the left is the weeping blue cedar (*Cedrus libani* ssp. *atlantica* 'Glauca Pendula').

Pale aruncus shows up the dark red roses that would otherwise merge into the background.

Rhododendron hybrids 'Golden Torch' and 'Sneezy' provide neat domes of brilliant colour.

Being spoilt for choice, however, can be a mixed blessing when it comes to selecting plants. So often a visit to the garden centre will tempt us to buy something merely because of its pretty flowers without regard to anything else, and the flowers may well have faded before we have found a home for such an impulsive, perhaps already regretted, purchase. Far better, when planning a new garden or changing an established one, to look at the site first and think of what kind we need, what we want it to do for us, how it will fit in. Bearing this in mind, the chapters of this book have been arranged to describe some of the most important ways in which we use these varied and versatile plants.

Deciding on which trees and shrubs are most suitable becomes easier also if thought is given to some of the main characteristics (apart from flowers, dealt with in Chapter 2) which account for such a great diversity.

Size

Here it is important to note the rate of growth as well as the ultimate height and spread. It is misleading, alas, that when picked up at the nursery or garden centre all the shrubs seem to fit nicely into the boot of the car and none of the trees are too large for the roof rack. It pays to find out what their ultimate intentions are!

Sometimes, of course, we do need a shrub to grow fast or we intend to train and trim it into a hedge anyway, but when a large tree suitable only for forests or parks is planted in a small garden, there may soon be only two solutions to the problems this can create: to get rid of the tree or to move house.

Size, particularly in relation to the extent of the garden and the scale of the planting, is of vital importance.

Shape and Habit

How trees and shrubs are best used depends so much on these. If there is need of a shady canopy to sit under on a lovely summer's day, it would quite obviously be foolish to cut down the old spreading apple tree and replace it with a typically pyramid-shaped conifer.

But there are many other shapes, and do we always consider them? Three different flowering cherries: one a slender upright column, the other a weeping tree and the third like an up- and outward-reaching vase. One of them makes a gentle accent, the other could look beautiful as a specimen in the lawn, the third would nicely preside at the back of a mixed border. Many shrubs form the familiar hummock, but there are others which arch, like the beauty bush (*Kolkwitzia amabilis*); which have a striking architectural appearance like the rhus; or which just spread on the ground – after all, the periwinkle and the ivy are shrubs too.

Habit can dictate where we plant our trees and shrubs. The bare trunks of some trees are especially beautiful and we make sure they can be seen; on the other hand, the leafless stems of a lilac or philadelphus are not very attractive and are best placed at the back of a border with other plants in front of them to act as petticoats.

Clipped yews show the value of strong evergreen shapes even in winter.

A planting of conifers in gravel that is effortless to maintain, yet full of variety and interest.

The choice of tree and shrubs with variegated or golden foliage has lightened this border.

A mixed border incorporating mainly evergreen shrubs — yews, rosemary, cistus and cotton lavender.

Leaves

The most obvious distinction relating to leaves is whether they all come off in the autumn or not – whether the plant is deciduous or evergreen – and the implications of this are equally obvious. Nonetheless, a few words of caution. For some purposes, such as hedging, ground cover, background planting, or even for providing a cheering sight out of the window on a dreary winter's day, the steady presence of evergreens is a distinct advantage; but the changing scene provided by deciduous plants is to be welcomed also – the fresh leaves as they emerge in spring, the glories of the autumn tints.

Leaf colour needs to be interesting but also restful. Greens can vary so much – from light to dark, from yellowish to bluish – and should not be overlooked as the most important of all the colours. There is a place for the delicate silvers and greys. Few of us can resist the exciting highlight of a bright yellow tree or shrub, or the beauty of a purple-leaved smoke tree, not to mention all the variegations, but they should always be used with discretion. Plants in a garden are not seen in isolation; they are part of a picture.

Less obvious than colour, but very important nonetheless, are the other ways in which leaves differ. They come in all shapes and sizes, from the needles of a pine to the almost plate-sized ones of a catalpa. The texture varies also, and this will affect how the plant looks. The smooth, polished leaves of a holly or choisya will reflect light and look shiny; the rough, sometimes hairy ones of a *Hydrangea aspera* do not, and so give quite a different impression.

A flowery combination: the pink *Cistus* 'Peggy Sammons' surrounded by lilac trumpets of penstemon.

Cultural requirements

We have so far considered the qualities of plants which we take into account when we choose them to suit ourselves. But will these plants grow for us? Some can be quite particular as to the acidity or alkalinity of the soil, its quality and composition (clay, loam, sandy, chalk), whether it is well drained or not; they may need a spot which is shady or in full sun; they may tolerate salt winds or pollution or they may not.

The last two chapters of this book deal with trees and shrubs for very special conditions or with special needs, but it pays at all times to consider the plants' requirements and, of course, however tolerant they are, they should be planted and subsequently looked after with care.

1. Shrubs and Trees to form the Garden

These are the plants which give the garden a permanent framework and design.

PLANTING *the* BOUNDARIES

HEDGES COME FIRST TO MIND. They form an ideal enclosure, giving privacy and seclusion, cheaper nowadays than walls and prettier than fences. They can vary from tall, narrow 'living walls', created by regular clipping of trees such as thuja, yew, holly, beech, hornbeam and hawthorn, to less formal wider barriers of shrubs, such as barberries, allowed to flower and berry.

The popular ***Cupressocyparis leylandii*** **(Leyland cypress)** forms this impressive bulwark. It is hardy and fast-growing but often planted where another, less vigorous, hedge would suit the surroundings better.

Prickly and thorny hedges can deter burglars and straying animals. *Berberis* × *stenophylla*, *Hippophaë rhamnoïdes*, holly and some roses are all excellent for such unwelcoming thickets.

Carpinus betulus **(Hornbeam)** can be clipped into a dense hedge up to 6m/20ft tall, no wider than 45cm/1½ft.

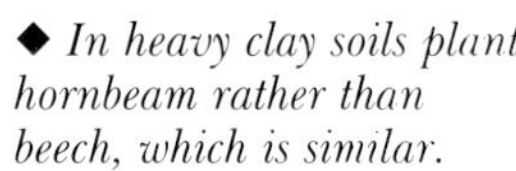

◆ *In heavy clay soils plant hornbeam rather than beech, which is similar.*

Fagus sylvatica **(Beech)** retains its attractive dead leaves in winter as does hornbeam. Prune both in mid to late summer.

Crataegus monogyna **(Hawthorn)** A deciduous tree more often associated with field hedges, is here neatly trimmed in midsummer to supplement the boundary wall.

◆ *The conifers within may be screening an ugly view or providing extra shelter.*

Trees and shrubs when allowed to grow naturally on garden boundaries form excellent screens and windbreaks. Suitable for shelter belts are conifers such as the **Serbian spruce (*Picea omorika*)** and hardy deciduous trees such as the **whitebeam (*Sorbus aria* 'Lutescens')** shown here.

Cotoneaster lacteus is a most amenable evergreen with long-lasting red berries. It makes a fast-growing screen for the smaller garden, easily cut back where necessary.

Creating *a* Framework

Boundaries merely outline a garden. By planting tall evergreen shrubs inside we can subdivide the usual rectangle into different areas, creating more interesting spaces not all seen at a glance.

Both straight lines and soft curves can be created with trees and shrubs. The promontory of taller plants here, forming a bay, is softened by lower foreground shrubs.

◆ *Internal hedges, of yew for instance, are well loved. Here conifers are used for a less formal structure.*

Illustrated here are some useful plants. ***Photinia* × *fraseri* 'Red Robin'** has attractive red new foliage and can reach 6 × 4m/20 × 13ft. ***Prunus lusitanica* (Portugal laurel)**, larger still, bears white flower spikes in early summer. ***Viburnum x burkwoodii* 'Park Farm Hybrid'** (3 × 2.4m/10 × 8ft) scents the garden throughout spring with its round white flower heads.

***Buxus sempervirens* (Box)** A low hedge here but could be 2m/6ft or more. Fully hardy, box grows in sun or deep shade. E, 5 × 5m/16 × 16ft

◆ *Hedges are greedy and need feeding so that nearby plants are not deprived.*

***Lavandula* 'Grappenhall'** Frost hardy. Lavenders are suitable for low hedges. Fragrant flowers mid/late summer. O, E, 1 × 1.5m/3 × 5ft

***Artemisia* 'Powis Castle'** Fine foliage shrub. Pruned hard in spring, it quickly regrows. O, E, 1 × 1.2m/3 × 4ft

***Santolina pinnata* ssp. *neapolitana* (Cotton lavender)** Ideal for edging or mass planting. Yellow flowers midsummer. O, E,. 75cm × 1m/2½ × 3ft

Creating *a* Framework

SMALLER GARDENS, as well as subdivided areas of larger ones, still need the permanent backbone planting of evergreens, not only as hedges or isolated groups. In a mixed border they give it shape and stability. They form a framework within which the transient flowers of other plants can come and go while the basic design remains.

***Cistus* × *aguilarii* 'Maculatus'** Flowers from early to midsummer. A somewhat tender shrub (also called rock rose). ❍, E, 1.2 × 1.2m/4 × 4ft

***Lonicera nitida* 'Baggesen's Gold'** Cheerful even in midwinter. The green form often used as hedging. E, 1.5 × 1.5m/5 × 5ft

***Escallonia* 'Apple Blossom'** For borders or hedges in mild areas. Flowers early to midsummer. Dark glossy leaves. ❍, E, 2 × 2.4m/ 6 × 8ft

***Juniperus sabina* 'Tamariscifolia'** The Savin juniper is valuable for dry banks or border edges. E, 1 × 2m/3 × 6ft

Euphorbia characias subsp. ***wulfenii*** Magnificent yellow-green flowers in spring. This spurge is effective on its own or in borders. E, 1 × 1m/3 × 3ft

***Brachyglottis* 'Sunshine'** (syn. *Senecio* 'Sunshine') Easily controlled shape, lovely foliage and yellow summer flowers. O, E, 1 × 1.5m/3 × 5ft

***Choisya ternata* (Mexican orange blossom)** Effective alone, in mixed borders or as low hedge. Worth protecting in cold areas. E, 2 × 2m/6 × 6ft

Evergreens are invaluable especially near the house or paths, where they are seen and appreciated throughout the year.

The grey-leaved plants on these pages prefer light, well-drained soil and full sun.

Cuttings from many shrubs root easily and will give you insurance against loss in a severe winter.

Sometimes a shrub is planted for its foliage. If the flowers offend, cut them off (as many gardeners do with santolina and brachyglottis).

Specimen Trees

***Salix caprea* 'Kilmarnock' (Kilmarnock willow)** A small weeping willow with grey catkins early to midspring. Makes a good specimen for a small garden. 2 × 2m/6 × 6ft

Weeping and horizontally-branched trees, in particular, need space to display their shape and habit.

***Abies koreana* (Korean fir)** Conical fir with attractive cones for a moist site. ◐, E, 8 × 5m/26 × 16ft

Rhus hirta (syn. *R. typhina*) Stag's-horn sumach renowned for its orange-red autumn foliage and interesting architectural shape. 5 × 6m/16 × 20ft

Sorbus vilmorinii Graceful small tree with delicate leaves turning orange and red in autumn. Pink fruits. 5 × 5m/16 × 16ft

Malus hupehensis Magnificent spring-flowering crab with deep green foliage and large scented white flowers. The crab apples that follow in autumn are yellow with a red tinge. 10m × 10m/ 33 × 33ft

***Sciadopitys verticillata* (Japanese umbrella pine)** A conical tree with red-brown bark and curiously whorled leaves. E, 13 × 2m/43 × 6ft

Specimen Trees

These form focal points within the framework and should have special qualities such as beautiful shape, flowers, foliage, bark or berries. Above all, their ultimate size must suit the setting.

***Pyrus salicifolia* 'Pendula'** Grey-leaved pear, mound-shaped and weeping. 7.5 × 7.5m/25 × 25ft

***Acer griseum* (Paper-bark maple)** Beautiful peeling bark, autumn colours and shape – a most desirable maple. 8 × 6m/26 × 20ft

***Betula pendula* 'Youngii'** Small, spreading, delicately-branched shade tree, weeping to the ground. 7.5 × 10m/25 × 33ft

◆ *Spring catkins and yellow autumn foliage are further attractions of many birches.*

Specimen Shrubs

Planted singly on a lawn any shrub would catch our attention – a favourite rose, perhaps. But distinctive shape, habit or leaf interest are some of the outstanding features which turn others into focal points, whatever the setting. They enhance and dominate their surroundings as trees do on a larger scale.

Abies balsamea* f. *hudsonia Slow-growing conifer with spirally arranged leaves. Attractive spring growth. For rock gardens. E, 1 × 1m/3 × 3ft

***Chamaecyparis lawsoniana* 'Minima Aurea'** Scale is important and amongst low planting this dwarf will provide year-round interest. E, 1.2 × 1.2m/4 × 4ft

Buddleja alternifolia Pruned here into a small weeping 'tree'. Lilac early-summer flowers. O, 4 × 4m/13 × 13ft

***Viburnum plicatum* 'Mariesii'** Horizontal branches with lace-cap flowers in late spring/early summer. 3 × 4m/10 × 13ft

***Magnolia stellata* (Star magnolia)** White star-shaped flowers in early spring. Slow growing but most worthwhile. 3 × 4m/ 10 × 13ft

◆ *Plant magnolias where morning sun cannot damage frosted flowers.*

SPECIMEN SHRUBS

These accent plants are best used sparingly; they should make the scene interesting but not restless.

Specimen shrubs need not be evergreen. Even leafless, their architecturally interesting skeleton is still effective.

Consider also *Kolkwitzia amabilis* (the beauty bush) 3 × 3m/10 × 10ft and *Rosa glauca* 2 × 1.5m/6 × 5ft. Both are deciduous, gracefully-arching shrubs.

***Chusquea culeou* (Chilean bamboo)** Stout stems slowly form a large clump of strong, upward-thrusting shape. E, 5 × 2.4m/16 × 8ft

Fargesia nitida (syn. *Sinarundinaria n.*) Small leaves, white with frost here, usually mid-green. Purple-stemmed bamboo of indefinite spread. E, 5m/15ft

***Juniperus communis* 'Compressa'** Diminutive conical form of common juniper. Dislikes wind and frost. E, 75 × 15cm/30 × 6in

Yucca filamentosa Lanceolate mid-grey leaves and long-lasting white flowers on tall panicles. ❍, E, 2 × 1.5m/6 × 5ft

***Phormium tenax* (New Zealand flax)** Sword-shaped leaves and panicles of bronze-red flowers. ❍, E, 2.4 × 1.5m/8 × 5ft

***Aralia elata* 'Variegata'** Impressively large leaves on this Japanese angelica tree. 3.5 × 3m/12 × 10ft

◆ *The white flowers appear late summer.*

Good Partners

Many of these shrubs can also be free-standing specimens, mass-planted or used for hedging.

Leafless in winter and early spring, deciduous shrubs are ideal for underplanting with favourite spring bulbs.

Eucalyptus gunnii and *Acer negundo* 'Flamingo', potentially trees, provide a shrub-like foliage effect when pruned regularly.

Deciduous shrubs, particularly those rounded in shape, blend and mix well if leaf colour is carefully considered. Their foliage, changing with the seasons, augments the more static evergreens in borders.

***Cotinus coggygria* 'Royal Purple' (Smoke tree)** Magnificent foliage turns bright red late autumn. Summer flowers. 4 × 4m/ 13 × 13ft

◆ *This bush makes a good background to pale pink and blue flowers.*

***Weigela florida* 'Foliis Purpureis'** Purple-green leaves and pink tubular flowers. 1.2 × 1.5m/ 4 × 5ft

***Rosa* 'Cornelia'** flowers all summer. Ideal for mixed borders. ○, 1.2 × 1.2m/ 4 × 4ft

◆ *Other valuable hybrid musk roses are: 'Buff Beauty' and 'Felicia'.*

***Cornus alba* 'Elegantissima'** This dogwood is normally a rounded bush but has been pruned here into a mop-head. 3 × 4m/10 × 13ft

***Spiraea* 'Arguta' (Bridal veil)** Gracefully arching with white spring flowers. Dainty leaves yellowing in autumn. 2.4 × 2.4m/8 × 8ft

GOOD PARTNERS

AGAINST THE BACKDROP of evergreen ***Elaeagnus* × *ebbingei*** and ground-covering × ***Fatshedera lizei***, ivies and perennials, these deciduous shrubs blend with the presiding tree, ***Gleditsia triacanthos* 'Sunburst'**. Yellow-leaved ***Philadelphus coronarius* 'Aureus'** and ***Physocarpus opulifolius* 'Aureus'** welcome light shade at the back, ***Hypericum* × *inodorum* 'Elstead'** and ***H.* 'Hidcote'** contribute with flowers, ***Spiraea japonica* 'Gold Flame'** and ***Diervilla sessilifolia*** with foliage towards the front. Green leaves of white-flowered ***Hydrangea quercifolia*** (left) and ***Viburnum opulus* 'Compactum'** (right) add interest and variety.

GROUND COVER *in* SHADE

SOME PLANTS, mostly evergreen, form a leafy weed-suppressing cover, whether they are low carpeting or taller. Not only utilitarian, they have landscaping value also, the low ones providing quiet flat areas to set off other plants.

Cotoneaster dammeri Has glossy leaves, white flowers and, later, bright red fruits. For medium shade. E, 30cm × 3m/12in × 10ft

◆ *Many cotoneasters are deep-rooting and excellent for binding soils on banks.*

Viburnum davidii has unusually bold, deeply veined leaves. The turquoise blue autumn berries are remarkable also. E, 90cm × 1.5m/3 × 5ft

Lonicera pileata Box-like leaves on low branches. Tolerates dry shade. E, 60cm × 2m/2 × 6ft.

Ground Cover *in* Shade

SHADE CONDITIONS VARY. Light intensity may be high by sunless walls, low under leafy trees, and the soil rich or poor, wet or dry. Luckily different plants thrive in different places.

***Vinca minor* 'Aureo-variegata'** Lesser periwinkles have white or purple flowers. Rapidly spreading trailers. E, 15cm/6in (spread indefinite)

***Mahonia aquifolium* (Oregon grape)** Not for dry soil. Has handsome glossy foliage, scented yellow spring flowers and autumn berries. E, 1 × 1.5m/3 × 5ft

***Rhamnus alaternus* 'Argenteovariegata'** This bushy buckthorn will tolerate semi-shade. E, 3 × 3m/10 × 10ft

***Euonymus fortunei* 'Emerald Gaiety'** Lively variegated foliage. Can climb or creep. E, 1 × 1.5m/3 × 5ft

***Hedera helix* 'Glacier'** The evergreen trailing shoots of ivy root as they spread, rapidly forming an attractive carpet.

◆ *Though tolerating wide-ranging conditions, ivies prefer semi-shade.*

Little maintenance is needed of plants on these pages, but plant in clean soil and weed carefully until established.

Existing overhanging shrubs or trees should not be threatened by competition; their roots are generally deeper.

Many shrubs brighten dark areas with flowers and berries as well as with their attractive foliage.

Euphorbia amygdaloides* var. *robbiae This spurge tolerates poor dry soil and semi-shade. Spring flowers. E, 60 × 60cm/2 × 2ft

Ground Cover *in the* Open

Many plants, such as heathers, are ideal for mass planting, and form restful, harmonious carpets.

Suitable conifers range from the low-growing spruce, *Picea abies* 'Procumbens', to the Pfitzer juniper ultimately 5m/16ft high.

***Hypericum calycinum* (Rose of Sharon)** Grows almost anywhere with yellow flowers throughout summer. Controls erosion on slopes. However, can be invasive and suffer from rust. E, 30cm/12in

***Rosa* 'Red Blanket'** Low shrub rose with glossy, healthy foliage, flowering repeatedly. 1.2 × 2m/4 × 6ft. 'Rosy Cushion' and 'Swany' are lower still and a light pink. 75 × 150cm/2½ × 5ft. Of easy maintenance as winter pruning can be done mechanically or with shears.

◆ *Prostrate sprawling roses form colourful carpets, like 'Nozomi' 30cm × 1.2m/1 × 4ft and the wider-spreading 'Max Graf' and 'Pheasant' 60cm × 3m/2 × 10ft.*

***Hebe pinguifolia* 'Pagei'** has fine glaucous leaves and white spring flowers. Will sprawl into neglected corners. E, 30cm × 1m/ 1 × 3ft

Erica carnea Easily maintained, these winter heaths will tolerate some lime and shade. E, 30 × 45cm/12 × 18in

◆ *Mulch heaths and heathers regularly with organic matter.*

Ground Cover *in the* Open

Where the garden needs a flat 'breathing space', lawns come first to mind. But they are far more labour intensive than some shrubs which not only fulfil the same function but are problem solvers for difficult positions such as steep banks and poor dry soil. Furthermore, the often interesting habit and colourful foliage of shrubs are valuable design and landscaping assets.

***Juniperus horizontalis* 'Wiltonii'**, sometimes called the Wilton carpet juniper or 'Blue Rug'. There are many creeping junipers, all hardy evergreens, loving sun and good drainage. Varying in growth rate and spread, their siting and spacing is important. Other cultivars include 'Bar Harbor', 'Douglasii', 'Plumosa', 'Blue Chip' and the Glauca group.

◆ Juniperus communis *'Repanda' and* J. procumbens *'Nana', also mat-forming, finally spread to 4m/13ft. Forms of* Juniperus × media *and* J. sabina *grow into taller and imposing landscape features.*

2. Interest through the Seasons

Careful planting can produce a succession of displays throughout the year.

Spring Trees

We are spoilt for choice because so many trees have beautiful spring foliage and flowers. Some, such as horse chestnuts and the tulip tree are too large, but others – particularly ornamental cherries, magnolias, crab apples and hawthorns, to name but a few – are suitable even for the smallest plot.

***Malus* 'Red Jade'** A small weeping tree whose white, pink-tinged flowers are followed by long-lasting red crab apples. Excellent specimen for a small lawn. 4 × 6m/13 × 20ft

***Sorbus aria* 'Lutescens'** The leaves of this whitebeam, silver-grey in spring, become green and white-backed later. 12 × 7m/ 39 × 23ft

***Prunus* 'Pink Shell'** An elegant ornamental cherry for those who prefer delicate to strong pink flowers. 9 × 8m/30 × 26ft

***Acer pseudoplatanus* 'Brilliantissimum'** The foliage later becomes yellow-green then green. 6 × 7m/20 × 23ft

Cercis siliquastrum The Judas tree bears pink flowers late spring and red pods later. ❍, 10 × 10m/ 33 × 33ft

***Crataegus laevigata* 'Paul's Scarlet'** Hawthorn with masses of double red flowers late spring. Glossy foliage. 6 × 7m/20 × 23ft

Cornus nuttallii Dogwood with tiny flowers and large white bracts in late spring. Not always long-lived. ❍, 13 × 8m/43 × 26ft

Magnolias are amongst the stateliest hardy trees, beautiful in flower and habit, though larger species take several years to flower (such as *M. kobus* and the evergreen *M. grandiflora*). Many prefer lime-free soil, but all tolerate heavy clay and atmospheric pollution.

***Magnolia* × *loebneri* 'Leonard Messel'** A lime-tolerant hybrid; flowers on bare branches mid-spring. 8 × 6m/26 × 20ft

Magnolia* × *soulangeana Deservedly popular, many clones are grown. This is 'Burgundy'. The magnificent flowers are produced even on young plants. ❍, 6 × 6m/ 20 × 20ft

SHRUBS WHICH ARE HARDY IN COOL CLIMATES tend to flower at this time, their beauty transforming the garden after the long winter. Many of them, especially viburnums and daphnes, are wonderfully fragrant.

Salix lanata The woolly willow is a sturdy little shrub often planted in rockeries although, like most willows, it enjoys moist soil. 1 × 1m/3 × 3ft

◆ Salix hastata *'Wehrhahnii' has attractive catkins also. Those of the much larger shrub* S. gracilistyla *'Melanostachys' are black.*

Osmanthus delavayi A valuable, highly fragrant shrub flowering mid to late spring. Small glossy, leathery leaves. E, 3 × 3m/10 × 10ft

Viburnum* × *juddii produces its sweetly scented flowers, pink in bud, freely from mid to late spring. 1.5 × 1.5m/5 × 5ft

◆ V. carlesii *and the larger* V. × burkwoodii *have similar strongly fragrant flowers.*

Spring Shrubs

***Chaenomeles speciosa* 'Nivalis'** A vigorous quince whose flowers, continuing throughout spring, are followed by large yellow fruits. A thorny shrub, taller than *C. japonica*, it lends itself to wall training, when side shoots should be cut back after flowering. 2.4 × 5m/8 × 16ft

***Photinia* × *fraseri* 'Red Robin'** has long-lasting brilliant red new foliage. Requires protection from cold winds. E, 6 × 4m/ 20 × 13ft.

***Magnolia liliiflora* 'Nigra'** flowers from mid-spring to midsummer. A beautiful, hardy, aristocratic shrub. 4 × 3m/12 × 10ft

Spring Shrubs

While many herbaceous plants still await their turn, shrubs – together with trees and bulbs – hold centre stage. Among those in flower are some like the firethorns and juneberries which star again with berries or foliage in autumn. Often shrubs, including evergreens, produce spectacular spring foliage which vies for our attention.

***Camellia* 'Rubescens Major'** An upward-growing, hardy japonica cultivar. Needs lime-free, humus-rich, cool, moist soil and protection. ◐, E, 3 × 3m/10 × 10ft

◆ *Camellias, beautiful all year, grow well in containers where conditions are easily controlled.*

***Daphne odora* 'Aureo-marginata'** has very early fragrant flowers. A gem needing protection and some shade. E, 1.5 × 1.5/5 × 5ft

Daphne mezereum Scented flowers appear before leaves late winter/early spring. 1.2 × 1.2m/4 × 4ft

Spring Shrubs

Rhododendrons are vastly important and not forgotten. They appear in Chapter 4, as do other acid-loving plants such as pieris.

Spring flowers cover a vast colour range. If we select and site them carefully, we can enjoy the variety without being offended by blatant clashes.

Ribes sanguineum 'Brocklebankii', 'King Edward IV' and 'Pulborough Scarlet' are some favourite flowering currants. 2 × 2m/6 × 6ft

Berberis darwinii Spiny shrub for borders, mass planting or hedges. Purple berries in autumn. E, 4 × 4m/13 × 13ft

***Prunus tenella* 'Firehill'** Resents pruning. *P.* × *cistena*, of similar size, has purple leaves and white flowers. O, 2 × 2m/6 × 6ft

◆ *One of these in a spring border will make it look furnished.*

Not only daffodils have yellow flowers in spring! Many shrubs do, including ***Kerria japonica*** (above), *Buddleja globosa*, *Azara serrata*, *Coronilla valentina* ssp. *glauca*, *Corylopsis pauciflora*, *Genista tinctoria*, *Ulex europaeus*, roses such as *R. xanthina* 'Canary Bird' and 'Frühlingsgold' and other berberis, cytisus and forsythias.

Chimonanthus praecox Aptly named wintersweet. Fragrant flowers produced from winter to early spring. ❍, 2.4 × 3m/8 × 10ft

Cytisus* × *kewensis. Low and arching, for walls, rock gardens or ground cover. Light prune only. ❍, 45cm × 1.5m/1½ × 5ft

Forsythia* × *intermedia Useful for hedging. (Best trimmed after early spring flowering). 3 × 2m/10 × 6ft

Early Summer

Having started flowering late spring, many shrubs such as *Rubus* 'Benenden' and *Viburnum plicatum* 'Mariesii' bridge the seasons. Among the lilacs and roses, cultivars take over from often earlier flowering species. Rhododendrons continue their display in gardens with acid soils.

***Ceanothus* 'Blue Mound'** A beautiful shrub which needs shelter as it is not fully hardy. ❍, E, 1.5 × 2m/5 × 6ft

◆ *Bold plants like this stand out well against paving or fussy backgrounds.*

The flowers of ***Syringa vulgaris* (common lilac)** cultivars are unsurpassed. Other lilacs may be preferred for elegance of foliage and habit. ❍, 6 × 4m/20 × 13ft

***Deutzia* × *elegantissima* 'Rosealind'** Beautiful shrub, as are white-flowered deutzias such as *D. gracilis*. 1 × 1.5m/3 × 5ft

EARLY SUMMER

THE GARDEN IS IN FULL SWING NOW with hostas and hardy geraniums at the feet of our shrubs, irises and peonies beside them. A time for many pinks and blues – softer than the vibrant colours of high summer – and the fresh green of shrubs and trees now in full leaf.

***Kolkwitzia amabilis* 'Pink Cloud'**, suitably named the beauty bush. Hardy, arching shrub for border and specimen planting. Tolerates most soils, prefers full sun. 3 × 3m/10 × 10ft

ROSES

Roses have been unchallenged favourites for centuries. Species roses and their close relatives are the first to flower. They are hardy shrubs which, needing little pruning, can develop their natural beautiful habit, shape, flowers, foliage and often hips.
Among those out in early summer: *Rosa moyesii*, *R. xanthina* 'Canary Bird', *R.* 'Nevada', the 'Frühlings' (spring) roses, *R. rugosa*. The Old French roses will start soon with Hybrid Teas, Floribundas, English roses and many more to follow.

'Graham Thomas' An English rose, which resembles the Old roses but flowers all summer. ❍, 1.2 × 1.2m/4 × 4ft.

'Fritz Nobis' A vigorous, early-flowering Modern shrub rose related to *R. rubiginosa*. ❍, 2 × 1.5m/6 × 5ft

'Lavender Pinnochio', a Floribunda rose, loved for its scent and beautifully coloured blooms.

Rosa glauca An original species, beautiful with or without its pretty flowers. 2 × 1.2m/6 × 4ft

Early Summer

The blossom of trees is not yet past. Some dogwoods, hawthorns and magnolias are still in flower, joined now by the beautiful snowbell trees, *Styrax americana* and *S. japonica*, by *Aesculus flava*, the sweet buckeye, and the robinias – *R. pseudoacacia* and the less familiar, smaller, pink-flowered *R.* × *slavinii* 'Hillieri', which is excellent where space is limited.

***Weigela florida* 'Variegata'** The foliage remains variegated and carries interest throughout summer. O, 1.5 × 1.5m/ 5 × 5ft

Dipelta floribunda is closely related to weigela and equally beautiful with pink fragrant flowers.

Recommended pruning for weigela and philadelphus: cut to ground level one third of old branches after flowering.

***Philadelphus* 'Belle Etoile'** One of the best mock oranges, this arching shrub is smaller than *P.* 'Virginal', taller than *P.* 'Manteau d'Hermine'. Abundantly produced white flowers have purple blotches at the base. ❍, 2.4 × 2.4m/8 × 8ft

◆ *The beautiful flowers of philadelphus are, above all, valued for the strong scent which fills the garden.*

***Exochorda* × *macrantha* 'The Bride'** Needs pruning immediately after flowering. ❍, 2.4 × 3m/8 × 10ft

Tall shrubs and trees add an important dimension to gardens and give variety to our experience. Because of their height they can obscure the view and make us wonder what is beyond. They let us move from sunlight to their shade, from open spaces to restricted ones, from looking down to looking up.

This laburnum tunnel performs a similar function, giving height, shade and restricted visibility. For smaller gardens, pergolas, covered in climbers, will do the same, taking even less room.

◆ *For maximum effect underplant laburnums with bulbs or herbaceous plants that flower at the same time.*

Paeonia delavayi* var. *ludlowii formerly *P. lutea l.* It is the largest tree peony with beautiful bright green foliage. ❍, 2.4 × 2.4m/8 × 8ft

◆ Paeonia suffruticosa, *the Moutan tree peonies, are also upright hardy shrubs. These are cultivars, often from Japan, all with exquisite flowers. ❍, 2.2 × 2.2m/7 × 7ft*

Though tolerant of most soils, all peonies benefit from a mulch of well-rotted manure.

MID-SUMMER

A time for dead-heading, for pruning Old French and Rambler roses, even for sawing off unwanted tree branches. (Scar tissue forms more readily now than in the winter.)

AT THIS TIME THE SHRUBS WHICH WERE HARD PRUNED IN SPRING come into their own. They include *Buddleja davidii* (butterfly bush), some clematis, deciduous ceanothus, roses and lavateras. For the valuable shrubby potentillas, hypericums and helianthemums this is but part of a long flowering season.

***Lavatera* 'Barnsley'**, given full sun and well-drained soil, will flower for months. Valuable even though not very hardy. Take cuttings as insurance. 2 × 1m/6 × 3ft

◆ Abutilon × suntense, *flowering somewhat earlier, also not fully hardy, is another fast-growing shrub easily propagated.*

***Ceanothus* × *delileanus* 'Gloire de Versailles'** A vigorous, bushy shrub flowering from now to autumn. The cultivar 'Henri Desfossé' has darker blue flowers. 2 × 2m/6 × 6ft

Genista aetnensis, the Mount Etna broom, presides over this border of blue and yellow flowers. It is a graceful deciduous large shrub or small tree. Also yellow-flowered but much smaller (1.2 × 1.2m/4 × 4ft) is the versatile shrub ***Hypericum* 'Hidcote'**. Light blue ***Ceanothus* × *delileanus* 'Gloire de Versailles'** (see opposite) is complemented by the lower-growing lavender (***Lavandula angustifolia* 'Hidcote')** which, like the hypericum, is named after a famous garden. Sprawling over its neighbours, the indigo ***Clematis* × *durandii*** is a cross between a shrubby and a herbacious species.

Late Summer Flowers

Some of the most valuable shrubs for late summer are the long-flowering kinds like potentilla and hypericum, which begin earlier in the summer. But it is the hydrangeas and fuchsias that are probably the most popular at this time. Most hydrangeas retain their flowers into autumn.

Hydrangea quercifolia The white panicles later turn pink and the beautiful leaves a vivid orange-red. A tolerant shrub but brittle-stemmed. 2 × 2.4m/6 × 8ft.

The Butterfly Bush

Buddleja davidii This beautiful, fast-growing shrub flowers best if hard pruned in spring. Popular and widely naturalised in the West now, it originally came from China, discovered there in 1869. 4 × 4m/13 × 13ft.

***Ceanothus* 'Autumnal Blue'** Though hardier than most, needs protection in cold areas. The deciduous ***Ceanothus* 'Gloire de Versailles'** also flowers now. ❍, E, 4 × 4m/13 × 13ft.

Late Summer Flowers

***Fuchsia* 'Margaret'** Hardy fuchsia in bloom from late summer till the frosts. Cut stems to base in spring. 1.2 × 1m/4 × 3ft.

Hydrangea villosa Spectacular lace-cap blooms. Prefers semi-shade and acid soil but will tolerate lime. 2.4 × 2m/8 × 6ft.

Indigofera heterantha in flower from mid-summer to autumn. A sun-lover excellent on dry sites. ❍, 2 × 2m/6 × 6ft.

Potentilla fruticosa Generously flowers all summer. Most useful shrub for ground cover, borders or banks. 1.2 × 1.2m/4 × 4ft.

***Hypericum* 'Rowallane'** Semi-evergreen and frost hardy, it will flower from mid-summer to late autumn. 1.5 × 1.5m/5 × 5ft.

Caryopteris × clandonensis Pruned to ground level each spring, grows quickly. Late, valuable blue flowers. ❍, 80 × 80cm/2½ × 2½ft.

Leycesteria formosa Also requires drastic spring pruning. The flowers are followed by shining purple fruits. 2 × 2m/6 × 6ft.

***Hibiscus syriacus* 'Blue Bird'** Produces a succession of flowers until mid-autumn. ❍, 2 × 2m/6 × 6ft.

◆ *Another blue-flowered shrub out now is* ***Perovskia atriplicifolia***.

AUTUMN FRUIT

MANY SHRUBS AND TREES make their greatest impact when smothered in fruits or berries. The cotoneasters and pyracanthas are perhaps the most impressive, but even plants grown mainly for their flowers like roses, crab apples and viburnums will brighten the garden with autumn fruits. Birds will share the feast of course, but do we really mind?

Rosa rugosa One of the healthiest, toughest of roses. Flowers are produced for months, often appearing together with bright red tomato-sized hips. ❍, 1.5 × 1.5m/5 × 5ft.

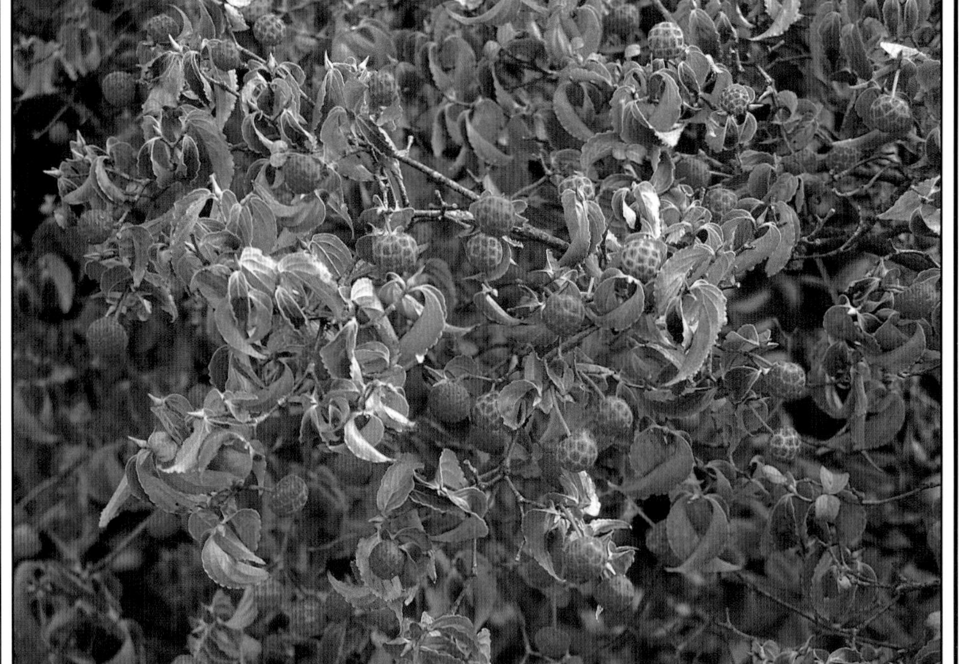

***Cornus kousa* (Chinese Dogwood)**. An elegant shrub. These fruits follow a wonderful summer display of white 'flowers'. 3.6 × 4m/12 × 13ft.

◆ *The flowers of dogwoods are themselves small but are set off by petal-like bracts.*

Chaenomeles Known more popularly as Japanese quinces or japonicas, these shrubs are easy to grow with beautiful spring flowers and autumn fruits. 3 × 3m/ 10 × 10ft.

AUTUMN FRUIT

***Viburnum opulus* 'Xanthocarpum'** Fast-growing and hardy. White lace-cap flowers followed by translucent berries. 4.5 × 4.5m/15 × 15ft

***Malus* 'Everest'** Pink-white flowers smother this dwarf crab apple in spring. Suitable for small gardens. 3.6 × 2.4,m/12 × 8ft

***Cotoneaster frigidus* 'Cornubia'** Semi-evergreen ideal screening shrub. Weighed down by its berries in autumn. 7 × 7m/23 × 23ft

◆ *The genus **Cotoneaster** includes dozens of valuable shrubs from tall to prostrate.*

***Pyracantha* (Firethorn)** Suitable for hedges and walls even in shade. Long-lasting berries. E, 4 × 3m/ 13 × 10ft

Callicarpa bodinieri var. ***geraldii*** Autumn brings purple foliage and these remarkable berries. 4 × 4m/ 13 × 13ft

Pernettya (Gaultheria) mucronata For acid soil. Different clones produce white, pink, red, purple or black fruits. ◐, E, 75 × 120cm/2½ × 4ft

***Arbutus unedo* (Killarney Strawberry Tree)** Though ericaceous, tolerates lime. Slow-growing handsome tree with gnarled trunk. Flowers and fruit appear simultaneously. E, 5 × 5m/16 × 16ft

Autumn Tints

The fall, so aptly named, brings with it one of the great spectacles of the year when nature's very own bonfire sets the dying leaves aflame. Maples and other great trees transform vast tracts of countryside. Our gardens, too, have their star performers, particularly the acers and sumachs.

Acer palmatum atropurpureum. Its bronzy purple foliage turns bright red. 4.5 × 4.5m/15 × 15ft.

◆ *All Japanese maples need protection from strong sun and cold winds.*

Rhus glabra* 'Laciniata'** 3 × 3m/10 × 10ft is a tough, wide shrub smaller than ***Rhus typhina. Both sumachs excel in the autumn.

◆ *Sumachs sucker freely. When pruning, beware of the irritating sap.*

Euonymus alatus slowly growing to 3 × 3m/10 × 10ft is best planted singly to show off its spreading habit.

The maple-like leaves of ***Liquidambar styraciflua*** appear only in late spring or early summer. 16 × 8m/52 × 26ft.

A Sheltered Spot

This corner is half-shaded by ***Malus tschonoskii***, one of the best crabs for autumn colour. ***Acer palmatum* 'Osakazuki'**, on the right, displays its fine leaves and shape against the background of ***Rosa rugosa* 'Alba'** which has turned a soft yellow. To the left, versatile ***Amelanchier* 'Ballerina'** adds vibrant oranges and reds whilst ***Hydrangea serrata* 'Preziosa'**, at their feet, tries to calm the scene with its more sombre purple tints.

WINTER FLOWERS

MANY PLANTS FLOWER AT THIS TIME. Place them where they can be seen and enjoyed. They will brighten the dreariest day, particularly if you have sited deciduous ones against a background of evergreens.

Mahonia japonica The sun has reddened the dark green pinnate leaves. A great architectural shrub with lax, lily of the valley-scented flowers. E, 3.5m × 3m/12 × 10ft

Garrya elliptica A bushy shrub which welcomes wall protection. The magnificent catkins last for many weeks. E, 4 × 3m/13 × 10ft

Jasminum nudiflorum **(Winter Jasmine)** is hardy, thriving almost anywhere. Its bare, green, whippy branches, covered in blossom, will brighten the dullest wall or bank. 3m/10ft

WINTER CARE

Tie back wall shrubs to prevent rocking in the wind.

Avoid pruning any shrubs that are not fully hardy during the winter. You could kill them.

Give doubtfully hardy shrubs a temporary cover of horticultural fleece.

Frost and gales can loosen plant roots. Refirm the soil and stake the plants.

Winter Flowers

THERE ARE MANY SHRUBS WITH FRAGRANT FLOWERS. They cannot be appreciated from afar or through a window of course. Planted near the front door, however, they give pleasure whenever one passes by, and hardly resent that the odd branch is picked for enjoyment indoors.

***Viburnum* × *bodnantense* 'Dawn'** A very frost-resistant shrub with small fragrant flowers. 3.5 × 3.5m/12 × 12ft.

***Viburnum tinus* 'Eve Price'** The pink flowers of this valuable shrub defy the frost from autumn to spring. E, 2.4 × 2.4m/8 × 8ft.

Hamamelis mollis The Chinese Witch Hazel, its spidery flowers richly scented. 5 × 6m/16 × 20ft.

Skimmia japonica Small, pollution-tolerant shrubs, thriving in most soils if given enough summer moisture. Their bright berries persist all winter. Male and female plants are required for pollination. E, 60 × 60cm/2 × 2ft.

◆ *Winter berries make excellent decorations in the house.*

Winter Bark *and* Stems

When the leaves have fallen from deciduous shrubs and trees we become more aware of their stems. Some of these have patterns and textures to engage our interest in the garden through the winter months.

***Cornus stolonifera* 'Flaviramea'** A vigorous spreading dogwood which contributes bright greenish-yellow stems to the winter garden. Small white flowers in early summer. 2 × 4m/ 6 × 12ft

◆ *Combine this plant with the red-stemmed dogwood (*Cornus alba*) for a colourful display throughout winter.*

Not only deciduous trees and shrubs have interesting barks. As well as the stone pine shown here there are many conifers that are worth growing for this reason.

***Pinus pinea* (Stone pine)** Slow-growing rugged pine with a flat head on a short trunk. 10 × 10m/33 × 33ft

◆ *This pine gives a picturesque Mediterranean effect to the garden.*

Acer capillipes One of the snake-bark maples, this has a green and white striped bark and coral new growths. 10 × 8m/33 × 26ft

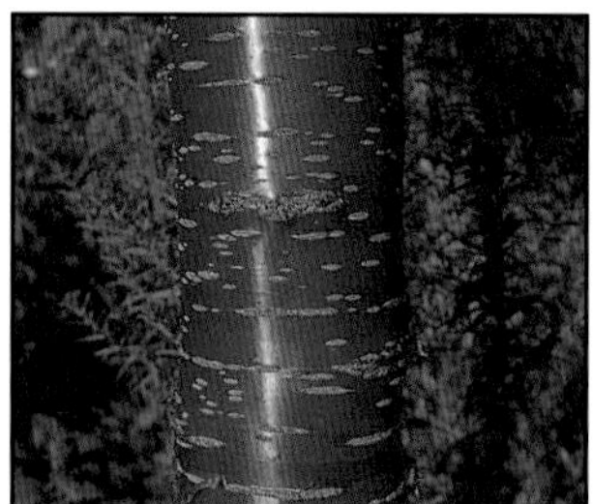

Prunus serrula A broad-headed cherry, grown for its shining red bark rather than its insignificant flowers. 9 × 9m/30 × 30ft

Betula utilis var. ***jacquemontii*** Ghostly white stems and a snowy, peeling trunk give this birch an outstanding presence. It has a broader outline than *Betula albosinensis* shown below which would be preferable where space is limited. 15 × 7m/49 × 23ft

Betula albosinensis var. ***septentrionalis*** This Chinese birch has a pinkish-orange, shining, peeling bark. Slim outline. 15 × 5m/49 × 16ft

3. Shrubs and Trees for Special Places

Selecting shrubs and trees which suit the conditions of your garden will make a successful scheme.

Purple-leaved ***Weigela florida* 'Foliis Purpureis'** is a slow-growing deciduous shrub rarely exceeding 1.2 × 1.5m/4 × 5ft. Its tubular pink flowers appear in late spring, early summer, as do the larger flower panicles belonging to the lilac ***Syringa* 'Antoine Buchner'**, an upright shrub – to 4m/13ft. Shown below is a branch of ***Cotoneaster horizontalis*** whose leaves turn red in autumn when the shrub is bedecked with bright red berries.

THIN SOIL *over* CHALK

THESE ARE DIFFICULT CONDITIONS which few plants prefer though many will tolerate. They include the Judas tree, *Cercis siliquastrum*, *Caragana arborescens*, the conifers *Pinus mugo* and *Taxus baccata* (yew). Cistus, deutzia, *Euonymus fortunei* and hebe will grow, as well as honeysuckle and mock orange (philadelphus). Berberis and cotoneasters are particularly valuable because they tolerate not only these but a wide range of soils.

The soil will be alkaline, so do not plant heathers or any member of the *Erica* family.

For hedges choose beech rather than hornbeam, which prefers a heavier soil.

Digging in plenty of humus will help water retention and adding vegetable matter repeatedly may in time lower the alkalinity.

Despite all efforts, fighting nature often leads to disappointment. Best to choose plants which grow well and plant others in containers or raised beds.

***Prunus* 'Kanzan'** One of the most popular of the Japanese ornamental cherries, all of which do well. The young leaves of this late-spring flowering tree are coppery red. 8 × 8m/26 × 26ft

Willows (*Salix* species) are well known and loved. Hardy and fast growing they often have attractive catkins and bark. *Salix gracilistyla* 'Melanostachys', *S. elaeagnos* and *S. hastata* 'Wehrhahnii' are large to medium-sized shrubs. *Salix exigua*, *S. daphnoides* and *S. caprea* 'Kilmarnock' are small trees suitable for gardens. However, many willows become very large. The famous weeping willow ***Salix* × *sepulcralis chrysocoma*** (shown here) may reach 25 × 25m/82 × 82ft if allowed to. It is often planted in too small a space.

***Salix alba vitellina* 'Britzensis'** This willow has been pollarded to keep it small. The new stems produced after cutting back last year's growth to within 5cm/2in of the trunk in early spring are bright red and make an attractive feature.

Damp Sites

Many more plants than those illustrated here thrive in damp (though not water-logged) soil, including alders and poplars among trees, neillia and symphoricarpus among shrubs, as well as bamboos.

Sorbaria tomentosa* var. *angustifolia (syn. ***aitchisonii***) Fast-growing, elegant and imposing, for single or mass planting or large borders. Flowers last midsummer to autumn. Yellow autumn foliage. Prefers sun. 3 × 3m/ 10 × 10ft

◆ *The enormous leaves backing the flower panicles in this picture belong to* Gunnera manicata, *a spectacular herbaceous plant.*

Hard pruning as recommended for the elder ensures larger leaves but may sacrifice flowers and berries.

Truly water-logged soil may need drainage, but some plants, including the conifer below, thrive in it.

Cornus alba Versatile shrubs grown for foliage and/or bright red winter stems. Often hard-pruned. 3 × 3m/10 × 10ft

***Sambucus racemosa* 'Plumosa Aurea'** Elder with outstanding yellow foliage if hard-pruned in spring, otherwise 3 × 3m/10 × 10ft.

◆ *Finely cut leaves (particularly if variegated) may scorch in strong sun.*

***Sciadopitys verticillata* (Japanese umbrella pine)** is small and wet tolerant. E, 13 × 2m/43 × 6ft

Hot Dry Places

Where plants originally come from often explains their likes and dislikes. Hot dry conditions suit many whose natural habitat is near the Mediterranean or in countries with similar climates. They rarely survive below –10°C/14°F, but where the soil is well drained they are invaluably tolerant of drought and hot sun.

Yucca gloriosa Sometimes called 'Spanish Dagger' – thanks to vicious leaf tips. E, trunk to 2m/6ft, midsummer – autumn flowers to 2.4m/8ft

***Cistus* 'Elma'** A sturdy bush with exceptionally large flowers in summer. The rock or sun roses do well on chalk and hate being transplanted. E, 2 × 2m/6 × 6ft

× *Halimiocistus* Flowers profusely late spring/summer. For rock gardens or front of border. E, 60cm × 1.2m/2 × 4ft

As is so often the case, not all plants with the same generic name have identical requirements. For example, *Cistus* × *hybridus* (formerly × *corbariensis*) and *C.* 'Silver Pink' are hardier than most other rock roses.

Phlomis fruticosa (Jerusalem sage) is also suitable, with whorls of golden flowers over grey-green leaves in early/midsummer. E, 1 × 1m/3 × 3ft

---

These plants are not used to a rich fare and need little feeding.

Hot Dry Places

Other suitable plants for hot areas include *Ruta graveolens* 'Jackman's Blue' (rue), *Erica arborea* (tree heath), *Hypericum calycinum* (Rose of Sharon) and many junipers.

Prune cistus and halimiocistus with care; they rarely shoot from old wood.

Extreme conditions have a garden design advantage: one cannot help but grow together plants which naturally associate well.

Cistus and helianthemum are both commonly known as rock or sun roses.

Ozothamnus rosmarinifolius Interesting, conifer-like, upright growth. Fragrant summer flowers displayed against dark foliage. E, 1.2 × 1.2m/4 × 4ft

Rosmarinus officinalis Aromatic foliage shrub flowering late spring/early summer. Has culinary and ornamental uses. E, 1.5 × 1.5m/5 × 5ft

Genista lydia This mounded broom which will trail over a rock is covered in yellow flowers in late spring and early summer. 60 × 60cm/2 × 2ft

Lupinus arboreus The tree lupin is a vigorous sprawling fairly short-lived shrub flowering in early summer. Semi-E, 1.5 × 1.5m/5 × 5ft

Lavandula Lavenders, for border fronts or low hedges, are much loved for scented flowers and foliage. E, 1 × 1m/3 × 3ft

***Artemisia* 'Powis Castle'** A vigorous sub-shrub grown for its delicate silver-grey foliage. E, 1 × 1.2m/3 × 4ft

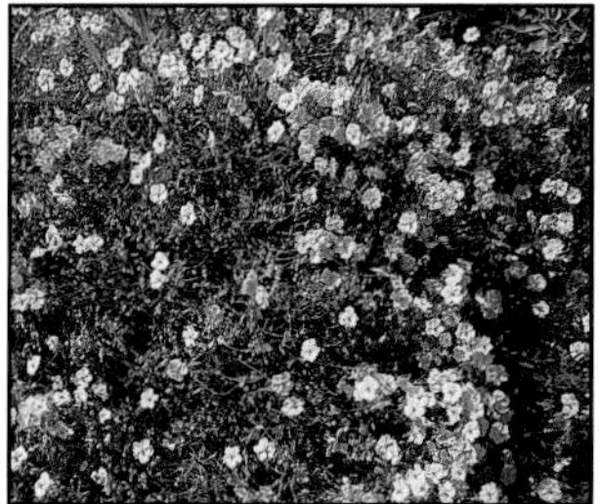

***Helianthemum* 'Golden Queen'** Many rock roses are fully hardy, flowering late spring to autumn. E, 30cm × 1m/1 × 3ft

Convolvulus cneorum has silky silvery leaves and blush-white funnel-type flowers. Tenderish and needs shelter. E, 60 × 60cm/2 × 2ft

Santolina pinnata ssp. ***neapolitana*** (**Cotton lavender**). Attractive grey foliage shrub. Yellow flowers midsummer. E, 75cm × 1m/2½ × 3ft

HEAVY SHADE

ALL THE PLANTS HERE share a tolerance of deep shade though they do not necessarily prefer it. However, they vary in other cultural requirements, of which soil conditions are perhaps the most important.

***Ruscus aculeatus* hermaphrodite (Butcher's broom)** Tolerates very dry conditions. Long-lasting berries. E, 1 × 1.2m/3 × 4ft

Sarcococca hookeriana* var. *digyna Deliciously scented winter flowers are followed by black fruits. Prefers leafy open soil. E, 1 × 1m/3 × 3ft

◆ *This sarcococca (sweet box) suckers but is not invasive.*

× *Fatshedera lizei* Grand foliage and interesting flowers best in moist soil. Can be trained up walls, etc. E, 2 × 3m/6 × 10ft

Variegated or shiny foliage, colourful flowers or berries are particularly welcome in otherwise dark places.

Some genera (e.g. *Ruscus* and *Skimmia*) are not usually 'self-sufficient': male and female plants are needed for berries.

***Aucuba japonica* 'Gold Dust'** Valuable stately plant bearing red berries autumn to spring. E, 2.4 × 2.4m/ 8 × 8ft

***Elaeagnus pungens* 'Dicksonii'** A framework shrub smaller than *E. p.* 'Maculata'. E, 2.4 × 3m/8 × 10ft

Fatsia japonica Large-leaved, prefers moist soil. Impressive and fast-growing. E, 3 × 3m/10 × 10ft

***Euonymus fortunei* 'Silver Queen'** One of many differently variegated trailing or climbing cultivars, tolerating dry soil. E, 2.4 × 1.5m/8 × 5ft

***Ligustrum ovalifolium* 'Aureum'** Useful privet for hedging and screening. Green and silver-variegated forms exist. E, 4 × 3m/ 13 × 10ft

Rubus tricolor This bramble's long stems form dense cover in deep shade. E, 60cm × 2m/2 × 6ft

***Skimmia japonica* 'Rubella'** White spring flowers follow red winter buds. For moist soil. E, 1.5 × 1.5m/5 × 5ft

Mahonia lomariifolia Not fully hardy, a true winter-flowering aristocrat. E, 3 × 2m/10 × 6ft

◆ *The magnificent yellow flowers of mahonias are very fragrant.*

The tree on the left, formerly *Tamarix pentandra*, is now ***T. ramosissima***. (Alas, plant names are often changed.) It has rose pink flowers in late summer and, like the bronze sword-shaped leaves of the **phormium**, happily withstands buffeting winds. The rose in front is a rugosa, **'Fru Dagmar Hastrup'**, whose ancestors grew on the seashores of Japan. On the right, evergreen ***Escallonia rubra* 'Crimson Spire'** backs ***Fuchsia* 'Riccartonii'**, often used for seaside hedges.

The Seaside

LIVING BY THE SEASIDE is a mixed blessing for plants. Whilst town dwellers need to withstand air pollution, inhabitants of coastal gardens must tolerate strong salt-laden winds unless protected by shelter belt planting of those which can. On the other hand, the climate is milder than nearby inland. Many plants thriving here may not be hardy in colder gardens. Holiday purchasers beware!

Leaves of the fast-growing shrub ***Griselinia littoralis***. Like the Holm oak (*Quercus ilex*) it is hardy in coastal areas and ideal for hedges and windbreaks. E, 3 × 2m/10 × 6ft

4. Shrubs and Trees with Special Needs

There is a range of desirable and beautiful shrubs and trees that require special conditions.

LIME-FREE SOIL

THE SO-CALLED 'LIME-HATERS' (or calcifuges) are plants which become malnourished and cannot thrive in alkaline soil: that is, soil high in calcium. Ericaceous plants like heathers belong in this group and so do some others.

Some magnolias tolerate lime, but most, including the beautiful ***M. salicifolia*** prefer neutral to acid soil. 10 × 5m/33 × 16ft

Soil-testing kits are cheap to buy and easy to use. They show whether soil is acid, neutral or alkaline and can save much disappointment and expense.

To change garden soil is difficult: one can add lime but not take it away. But many plants grow well in containers where special soil can be used.

***Nyssa sylvatica* (Tupelo)**
Attractive slow-growing tree with spectacular red and yellow autumn foliage. For sun and moist soil. Resents disturbance, so plant young. 16 × 12m/52 × 39ft

◆ *Another native of North America for similar conditions is the beautiful small tree* Halesia monticola *(Snowdrop tree).*

Leucothoë fontanesiana
Prefers shade and is excellent for underplanting. Racemes of white flowers mid/late spring, red-purple foliage in autumn. *L.f.* 'Rainbow' has pink/cream variegated leaves. E, 1.5 × 3m/5 × 10ft

LIME-FREE SOIL

***Calluna vulgaris* 'Silver Knight'** Excellent ground cover in full sun. Lings flower midsummer to early autumn. E, 40cm × 1m/ 16in × 3ft

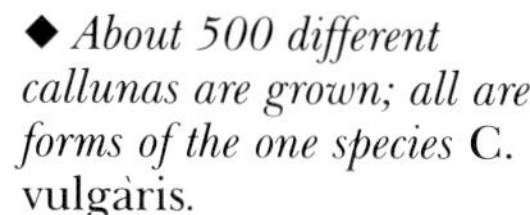

◆ *About 500 different callunas are grown; all are forms of the one species* C. vulgaris.

***Erica vagans* 'Lyonesse'** flowers midsummer/ autumn. It is very intolerant of drought. O, E, 75 × 75cm/2½ × 2½ft

Enkianthus campanulatus Woodland shrub with beautiful late spring flowers and spectacular red and yellow autumn foliage. 3 × 3m/10 × 10ft

***Kalmia latifolia* 'Nimuck Red Bud'** produces beautiful spring flowers a few years after planting. Full sun, moist rich soil. E, 3 × 3m/10 × 10ft

Cornus canadensis In shade, it forms a ground-covering carpet. Semi-E, H 20cm/8in.

◆ *Creeping dogwoods spread rapidly by underground runners, so plant 30cm/1ft apart in open leafy or sandy soil.*

Fothergilla major Fragrant spring flowers and vivid orange-scarlet autumn foliage. 3 × 3m/10 × 10ft

***Pieris* 'Forest Flame'** The red new foliage in spring (later turning pink, cream, finally green) needs protection from late frosts. *P. formosa* and *P. japonica* cultivars are equally beautiful. ◐, E, 2 × 4m/ 6 × 13ft

Rhododendrons prefer light shade but will tolerate full sun to medium shade if they are given enough moisture.

Different kinds of rhododendron flower from spring to early summer. Their flamboyant colours should be mixed with great care.

The best planting time is autumn. These shrubs are surface rooting, so do not plant too deeply and mulch rather than hoe.

RHODODENDRONS (WHICH INCLUDE AZALEAS) constitute a vast genus of flowering shrubs famed for their beautiful blossom. Mostly hardy and otherwise not difficult to grow, they must be planted in neutral to acid soil, preferably well-drained and rich in humus.

***R.* Hybrid 'Bric-a-Brac'** Flowers late winter/early spring. Flowers are vulnerable to frosts outside. E, 1.5 × 1.5m/5 × 5ft

***R.* Hybrid 'Lem's Cameo'** The flowers, pink in bud, appear mid-spring. Needs extra care and shelter. E, 2 × 2m/6 × 6ft

***R.* Azalea 'Hino-mayo'** Very floriferous, this evergreen forms a compact bush covered by small flowers in late spring. Tolerant of sun, it can be grown in containers for patio or conservatory use as well as in the garden. E, 1.5 × 1.5m/5 × 5ft

Literally thousands of different rhododendrons are grown. Most, though not all, are evergreen and their sizes range from dwarf to tree-like. Illustrated here are some smaller ones which, given the right conditions, are suitable for any garden, whatever its size.

Central to the picture are the great blood-red flowers (7.5cm/3in across) of the evergreen Hybrid 'Elizabeth' which slowly grows to 1.2m/4ft.

Above, on the left, are the remarkable flowers of the exceptionally hardy Hybrid 'Peeping Tom', a dwarf evergreen which flowers in mid to late spring.

The white flowers on the right belong to Azalea 'Palestrina', a floriferous and hardy evergreen growing to 1.2m/4ft, flowering late spring.

The pink flowers (bottom left) are a close-up of *R.* Azalea 'Hino-mayo' featured in the lower photograph, whilst on the right is pink *R. yakushimanum*, an outstanding semi-dwarf species, evergreen and of compact habit, 1 × 1.5m/ 3 × 5ft. The flowers, produced in masses late spring, fade to white.

Rhododendrons

IN NEED *of* WARMTH

THESE PLANTS ARE NOT HARDY below –10°C/14°F, or in some cases below –5°C/23°F. In colder gardens they should be placed in a sunny sheltered spot or grown up against a heat-retaining wall.

Carpenteria californica Bright green glossy foliage perfectly displays the white fragrant flowers in midsummer. E, 1.5 × 1.5m/5 × 5ft

◆ *If damaged by frost; carpenterias regenerate from old wood, even if cut back to ground level.*

***Cordyline australis* (New Zealand cabbage palm)** Usually grown as a specimen shrub suitable for containers. E, 1.5 × 1.5m/ 5 × 5ft

Abutilon megapotamicum Flowers late summer/early autumn. Its arching stems need support. 3 × 3m/ 10 × 10ft

IN NEED *of* WARMTH

Magnolia grandiflora Beautiful trees with large fragrant summer flowers and leathery leaves, shiny on top, felted beneath. E, 10 × 10m/33 × 33ft

***Cistus* 'Peggy Sammons'** A lovely combination of grey-green foliage and a succession of pink summer flowers. E, 1.2 × 1.2m/ 4 × 4ft

***Cytisus battandieri* (Moroccan broom)** Has midsummer, scented flowers and silken, silvery leaves. Semi-E 5 × 5m/16 × 16ft

***Escallonia* 'Iveyi'** Vigorous hybrid which spreads with age. Glossy leaves and flowers mid to late summer. E 4 × 3m/13 × 10ft

Myrtus communis (Common myrtle) Aromatic foliage shrub with fragrant flowers followed by black berries. Excellent for seaside. E, 3 × 3m/10 × 10ft

***Ceanothus* 'Concha'** This Californian lilac has small leaves and intensely blue spring flowers. E, 2 × 3m/ 6 × 10ft

***Fremontodendron californicum* (Flannel flower)** Beautiful fast-growing shrub which flowers spring to autumn. E, 6 × 4m/20 × 13ft

***Abelia* 'Edward Goucher'** Arching shrub with fragrant late-summer flowers. Semi-E, 1.5 × 1.5m/5 × 5ft

Itea ilicifolia The delicate drooping flower tassels are produced in late summer/early autumn. E, 3 × 3m/10 × 10ft

***Laurus nobilis* (Bay tree)** Often grown as a clipped specimen. The aromatic leathery leaves are used in cooking. Creamy-yellow flowers appear on male plants in spring. E, 12 × 10m/39 × 33ft

IN NEED *of* SHELTER *and* SOME SHADE

THE ANCESTORS OF MOST PLANTS HERE were woodlanders, so they have much in common, such as needing shelter from cold winds. However, they differ as to why and when they require shade. Acers, for instance, need protection from sun at mid-day whilst camellias in flower are vulnerable to early morning sun if they have been frosted overnight. Gardens which do not provide natural conditions for these plants can be made suitable by clever framework planting of trees and evergreens.

***Hydrangea macrophylla* 'Veitchii'** Among the hardiest and most lime-tolerant lace-caps. White outer florets fade to pink. 2 × 2.7m/6 × 9ft

***Hydrangea anomala* ssp. *petiolaris*.** Very hardy climbing or groundcover plant for all soil and sun/shade conditions. 1 × 15m/3 × 49ft

***Hydrangea macrophylla* 'Ayesha'** has fragrant mop-head flowers. 1 × 1.5m/3 × 5ft

***Hydrangea macrophylla* 'Hamburg'** Hortensia with pink-rose flowers on alkaline soil, purple-rose on acid. 2 × 2.4m/6 × 8ft

HYDRANGEAS

Hydrangea aspera and *H. paniculata* are but two of several loved species, but most popularly grown are the mop-headed 'Hortensia' and 'Lace-cap' descendants of *H. macrophylla* and *H. serrata*. They like semi-shade, neutral to acid soil and are particularly good near the sea. Their flowers, often pink in alkaline soil, blue in acid, are produced in late summer/autumn and are beautiful even when dry.

Acer palmatum* var. *dissectum Best in dappled shade and protected from spring frosts. The dark-leaved form shown here is called 'Atropurpureum'. 1.5 × 2.4m/5 × 8ft

In Need *of* Shelter *and* Some Shade

Cornus kousa bears small flowers surrounded by large bracts for a long period in early summer. 7 × 5m/ 23 × 16ft

Eucryphia* × *nymansensis Magnificent late-summer flowering tree. Needs its roots shaded and protection from cold winds. E, 15 × 4m/49 × 13ft

***Hamamelis* × *intermedia* 'Primavera'** Valuable fragrant winter-flowering witch hazel for light shade. Good autumn colour. 4 × 4m/13 × 13ft

***Acer shirasawanum aureum* (Golden leaved Japanese maple)** A beautiful shrub liable to scorch in full midsummer sun. 3 × 2.4m/10 × 8ft

Camellias

Camellias, hardy in all but the coldest gardens, are beautiful all year, with glossy evergreen foliage and sumptuous spring flowers. They need moist, lime-free soil and a sheltered position shaded lightly, particularly from early morning sun. Those grown include hundreds of *C. japonica* cultivars and excellent hybrids (involving other species, particularly *C. saluenensis* and *C. reticulata*) of which the *x williamsii* group is best known. The hybrids are often hardier, more floriferous and shed dead flower-heads naturally.

***Camellia* 'Konronkoku' (syn. *C.* 'Kouron-jura')** Medium-sized shrub with particularly frost-resistant semi-double flowers. E, 2 × 2m/6 × 6ft

***Camellia* 'Leonard Messel'** Vigorous, hardy hybrid (*reticulata* × *williamsii*) with semi-double flowers in mid-season. E, 3 × 3m/10 × 10ft

***Camellia* 'Galaxie'** A twiggy bush which produces masses of flowers. E, 2 × 2m/6 × 6ft

***Camellia* 'Nobilissima'** A japonica cultivar of upright growth, flowering very early. E, 3 × 2m/10 × 6ft